ROUTES

TO

SIGHT READING

FOR

GUITARISTS

Book One
by
Chaz Hart

**A CIP record for this publication
is available from the British Library**

ISBN: 1-898466-17-3

Published in Great Britain by

Registry Publications Ltd
Registry Mews, 11-13 Wilton Road, Bexhill, Sussex, TN40 1HY

Printed and bound in Great Britain by Gemini Press

INTRODUCTION

If you're interested in learning to read music - whether for classical, acoustic or electric guitar - then this book is for you! Starting at total beginner stage, the book takes you on a musical journey. You'll be guided on a route where you'll learn the notes on the guitar very gradually; progressing string by string. This way your musical journey should never be daunting. If you follow each path that's laid out in the book, without skipping any stages, you should never lose your way. By the end of the journey you'll be able to read the notes on the first few frets of all the strings, and you'll be familiar with most common musical rhythms and note timings. In other words, you'll be well on the road to becoming a fluent sight reader on guitar.

Studying this book with a teacher

This book can be used as a learning method for individual study. However, if you have a teacher to help you along the way than you'll find that the book has enhanced benefits:

Below each line of music a chord sequence is given. If you're learning *electric* guitar, ask your teacher to play these chords whilst you play the 'Guitar 1' melody – this will help you keep in time and bring the music alive.

If you're learning *classical* guitar, then you can play each piece as a duet with your teacher. You should play 'Guitar 1' (always printed on the left hand page) whilst your guitar teacher plays the music marked 'Guitar 2' (always printed on the facing right hand page).

Please note that whilst both the chords and 'Guitar 1', and 'Guitar 1' and 'Guitar 2', are designed to harmonise together, the chords and 'Guitar 2' are not intended to be played together.

Further on down the road

Once you've completed all the pieces in this book you should progress to the next volume in this series. It covers a wider range of keys and time signatures and guides you to the higher reaches of the fingerboard. You're bound to enjoy the journey!

To obtain the other books in this series ask in your local music store or contact:
Registry Publications on **01424 22 22 22** or buy on-line at:
www.BooksForGuitar.com

The Notes

These are the notes that are the foundation of your sight reading. They are shown on the musical stave, and underneath and alongside are the guitar strings and the fret numbers showing where the notes are played. In this *first position,* finger one will press at fret one, finger two will press at fret two, and finger three will press at fret three; this makes it easier to play accurately without looking. If you keep looking at the fingerboard, whilst you are trying to sight read, you will almost certainly lose your place in the music.

Note Values

The diagram below shows the length of different types of notes.

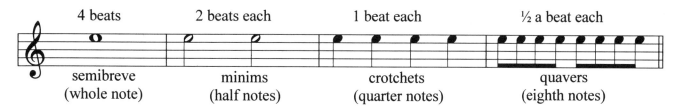

Time Signatures

The two numbers at the beginning of a piece of music are called the *time signature.* The top number indicates the number of beats in each bar that you need to count. The bottom number indicates the value of each beat. Shown below are the most common types of time signature:

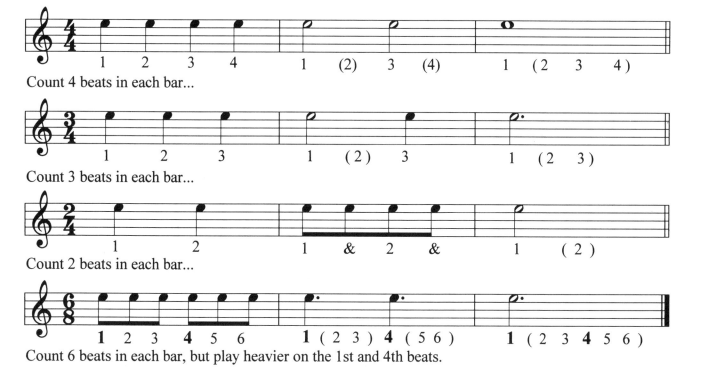

Count 4 beats in each bar...

Count 3 beats in each bar...

Count 2 beats in each bar...

Count 6 beats in each bar, but play heavier on the 1st and 4th beats.

3

1st String Notes

So here we go – your first step on the route to fluent sight reading begins now.

If you have never read a note in your life – DON'T WORRY! As long as you can count from 1 to 4 you can start to read music.

Much music is in $\frac{4}{4}$ time, so all you do is count 4 beats for each bar. e.g...

Count...   1   2   3   4   1   2   3   4

To try this first piece, all you need to know are these three notes that are all on the first string...
The numbers indicate the left hand fingering, and also the fret number to press at. ('0' means open string)

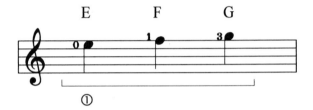

Avenue

Guitar 1.

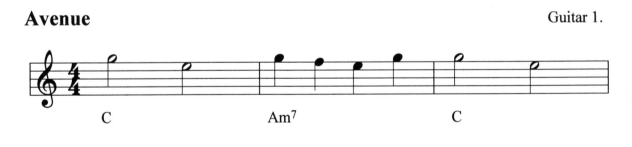

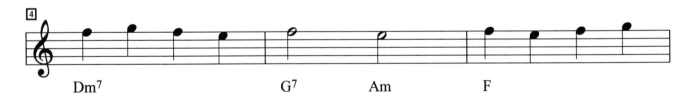

Tips for 1st Guitar

If you see a minim (ie. a half note, that lasts for 2 beats) still count to 4, but count the numbers in brackets under your breath and don't play on these beats – just let the previous note ring on.

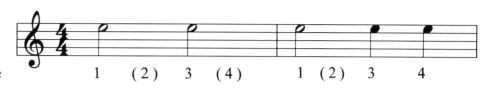

1 (2) 3 (4) 1 (2) 3 4

A semibreve (whole note) lasts for 4 beats. Count to 4 but only say the '1' loudly, and play on this beat. Make sure you let the note ring whilst you quietly count 2, 3, 4. The crotchets (quarter notes) are counted and played on each beat.

1 (2 3 4) 1 (2) 3 (4) 1 2 3 4

Never choose too fast a tempo when sightreading. Select a speed at which you can play the quickest note. Try to count and play evenly. If the music is in time, the tune will come through – regardless of the tempo.

Avenue

Guitar 2.

Fairfax Road

E   Dm   C

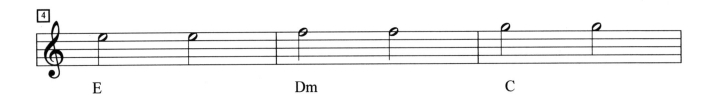

E   Dm   C

F   E   C

G   F   C

F   G   F   C

This piece uses the same three notes as 'Avenue' on the previous page.

Keep your left hand in position with your 1st and 3rd fingers over frets 1 and 3 in readiness for the notes that they play. Once you start playing try not to watch your left hand. Instead try and develop a sense of 'feel' for the position so that your fingers just touch the side of the frets.

Fairfax Road

Practise all the pieces with the aim of producing a clear sound and even timing.

Do not attempt further pieces until each stage is mastered.

Do keep the 1 – 2 – 3 – 4 rhythm regular and even.

Quavers (eighth notes)

Quavers (eighth notes) are played twice as quickly as crotchets (quarter notes). Say the word 'and' between the main beats to count the quavers...

1 and 2 and 3 and 4 and

Bushy Park

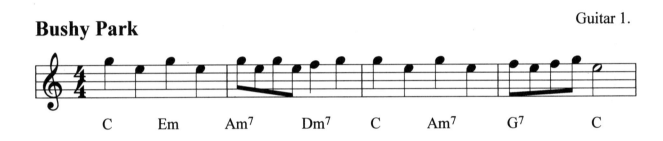

C   Em   Am⁷   Dm⁷   C   Am⁷   G⁷   C

Dm⁷   C   Dm⁷ Em C   Am⁷   G⁷   C

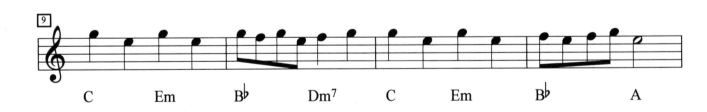

C   Em   B♭   Dm⁷   C   Em   B♭   A

A♭   G   F   G   C   Em   B♭   A

Tips for 1st Guitar

'Bushy Park' contains rhythms like this:

Practise this on a single string, before attempting to play 'Bushy Park', and remember to count.
IF YOU CAN SAY IT – YOU CAN PLAY IT!

Bushy Park

Guitar 2.

Dotted & Tied Notes

When a note has a dot after it, this increases the length of the note by half of its original value. So a dotted £10 note would be worth £15!

In this piece, the dotted notes are at the beginning of some bars. The dot itself falls on beat two – so count this beat quietly to yourself but do not play on it.

Ferry

E   Em^7 A   E

1 (2) & 3 (4)   1 (2) & 3   4

Amaj^7 Cmaj^7 Fmaj^7 E

1 (2) & 3 (4)   1   2 & (3) & 4

E$^{(add9)}$ Amaj^7 G^6 Cmaj^7

Fmaj^7 D^9 E

Tips for 1st Guitar

A curved line joining two notes of the same pitch is called a 'tie'. It is the technique for making the first note last longer than its normal duration.

When notes are tied together the second note is not played – instead it is allowed to ring on for the value of both the tied notes combined.

Notice that bars 9 and 10 will be played exactly the same as bars 5 and 6 – because a dotted crotchet (dotted quarter note) lasts the same length as a crotchet (quarter note) tied to a quaver (eighth note). Try counting out and tapping the rhythms before attempting the whole piece. Don't forget – SAY IT AND PLAY IT!

Ferry

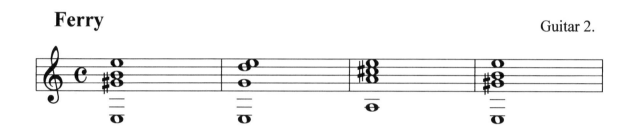

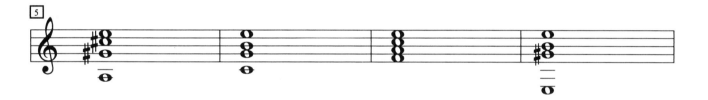

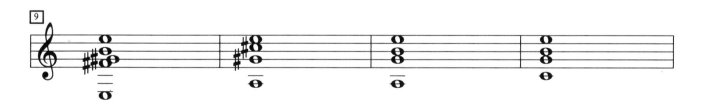

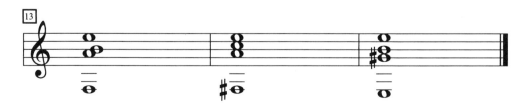

Tips for 1st Guitar

By now you should be able to play the three notes of E, F and G standing on your head, although I don't suggest you try that yet! Instead try another melody that uses a dotted rhythm.

To practise playing the dotted crotchet (dotted quarter note), that has the value of one and a half crotchet (quarter note) beats, try playing this top line first.

The last bar is the same rhythm as bar 9 of 'Strawberry Hill'.

Strawberry Hill

Guitar 1.

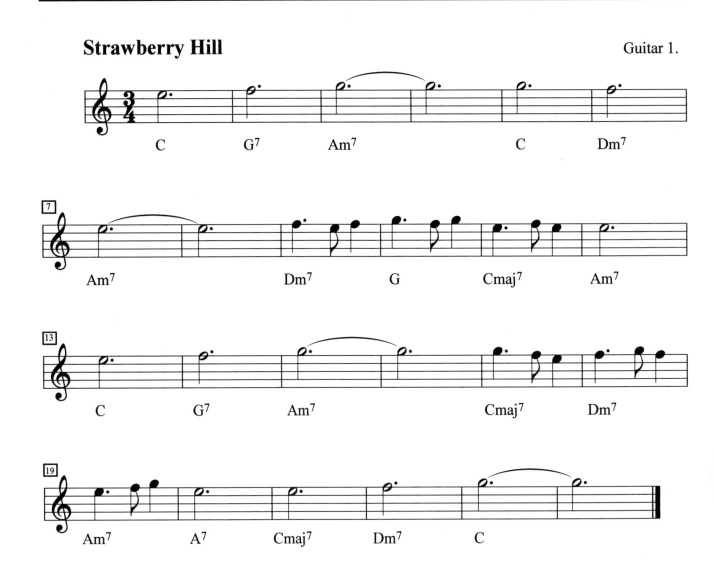

Make sure that you can count and tap this rhythm fluently and easily before attempting
'Strawberry Hill'.

Strawberry Hill

2nd String Notes

Now we start to play on the 2nd string.

The same three fingers are used as on the 1st string notes.

These are the notes for the 2nd string...

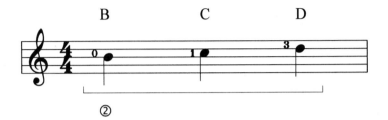

The timing of this piece is $\frac{2}{4}$ time – so you will only be counting 1 – 2 – for each bar.

Eel Pie

Guitar 1.

C   G   Am   Em

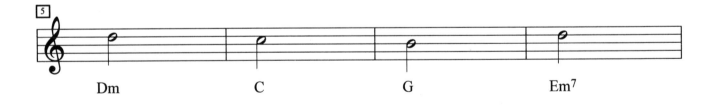

Dm   C   G   Em⁷

D⁷   G⁷   C

Reminder of the note values so far:

Semibreve – whole note   Minim – half note   Crotchet – quarter note   Quaver – eighth note

Strive for quality of tone by keeping the left-hand fingers close to the frets.

Press firmly with the tips of your left-hand fingers.

Don't overgrip the guitar neck with your thumb.

Eel Pie

Guitar 2.

Here are two more pieces using the 2nd string notes.

Watch out for the tied notes in 'Marble Hill'.

St. Margarets

Guitar 1.

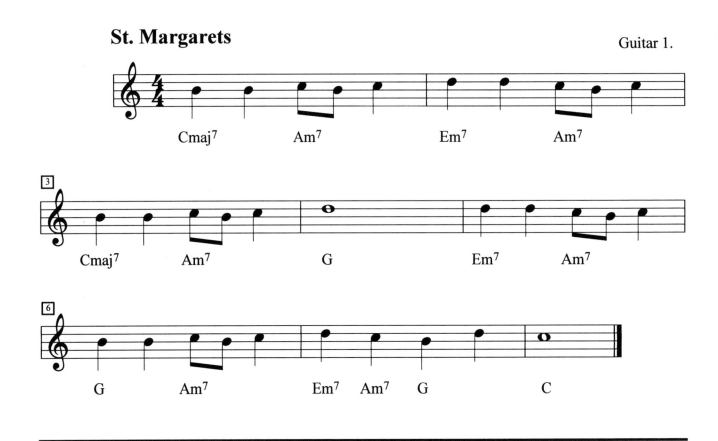

Marble Hill

Guitar 1.

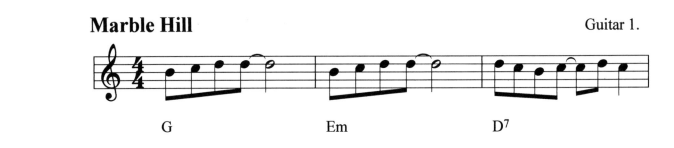

St. Margarets

Guitar 2.

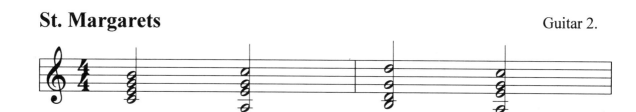

Marble Hill

Guitar 2.

Practise the difficult bars

Most pieces contain only one or two difficult rhythmic bars. The secret of a good sight reader is to notice these quickly, and practise counting them, before starting to play.

In this piece bars three and seven contain the difficult timing, so warm up by practising this exercise a few times:

Ducks Walk

Guitar 1.

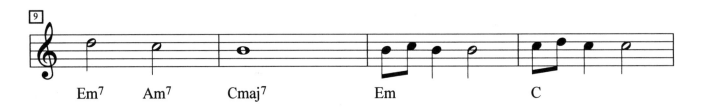

Summary of Notes

Practise the 6 notes that you have learnt so far by playing up and down them several times each day.
This will be a good preparation for the music that comes on the following pages – 'Richmond Green'
(on the following page) includes notes on both the 1st and 2nd strings.

Your six notes look like this:

Ducks Walk

Guitar 2.

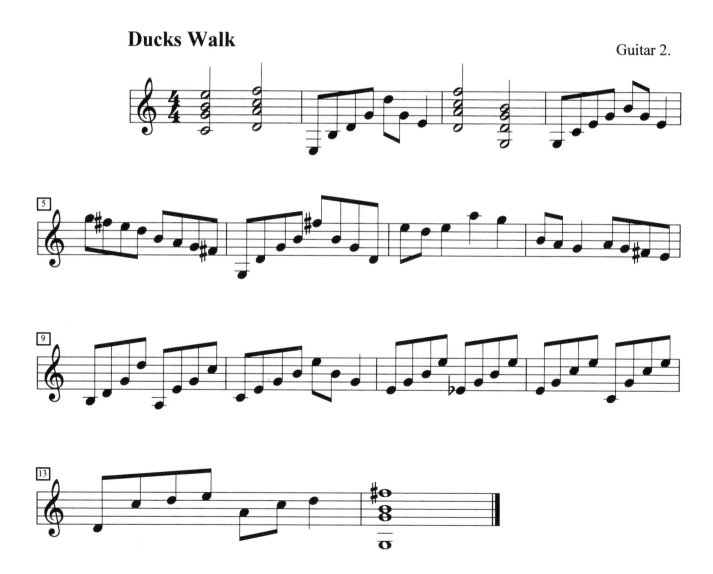

Combining 1st & 2nd String Notes

Richmond Green

Richmond Green

Guitar 2.

21

The Dotted Quaver & Semiquaver

This piece introduces the use of a dotted quaver (worth one and a half times a normal quaver) plus a semiquaver (twice the speed of a quaver).

Before attempting this, practise counting the semiquavers ($\frac{1}{16}$th notes) on the top of the next page.

Count: 1 & 2 & 3 & a 4 & a

Sandycomb

Guitar 1.

Dm Am F Dm

C Dm Am

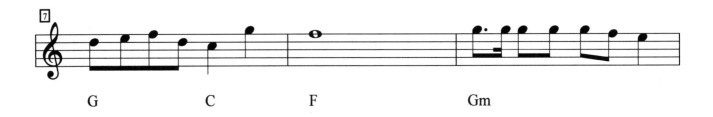

G C F Gm

Dm A7 Dm C7

F Dm Am C7 F

Crotchet – 1 beat	=	Quaver – ½ a crotchet beat	=	Semiquaver – ¼ of a crotchet beat. Good value – 4 for the price of 1!

Practise counting these notes before playing the piece:

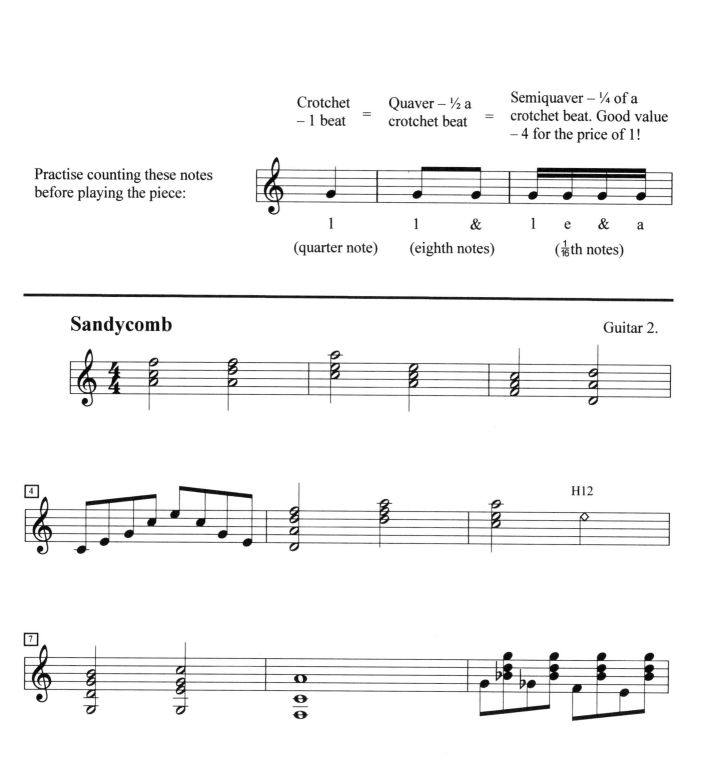

1   1   &   1   e   &   a

(quarter note)   (eighth notes)   ($\frac{1}{16}$th notes)

Sandycomb

Guitar 2.

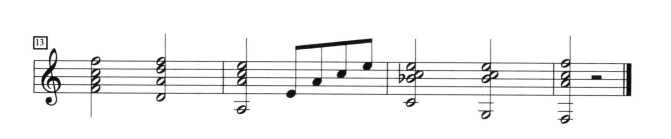

This piece contains all of the six notes that you have learnt. Memorise the first four notes of the tune before you start, then try to always look ahead. Being able to see a few notes in advance is one of the main *routes* to being a good *sightreader*.
Also, strive to accent the first beat of the bar – otherwise the rhythm can become bland.

Kew Bridge

Guitar 1.

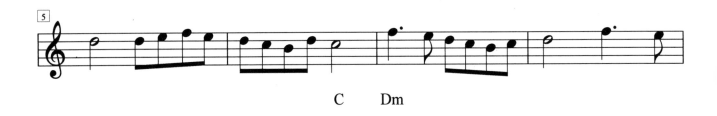

24

Kew Bridge

Guitar 2.

3rd String Notes

Here are the notes for the 3rd string...

If you have any problems with the timing in 'Silver Crescent', return to the section on dotted notes.

The **C** at the beginning of the piece is in place of the usual two numbers as the time signature. This is a short way of writing $\frac{4}{4}$ time.

Silver Crescent

Guitar 1.

Summary of notes learnt so far.

Practise these notes several times daily:

Silver Crescent

Guitar 2.

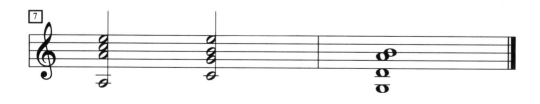

Combining Strings 1 to 3

The *'D.C. al Fine'* sign means start back at the beginning and play up until the sign –*'Fine'* (The End).

Dukes Avenue

Guitar 1.

Dukes Avenue

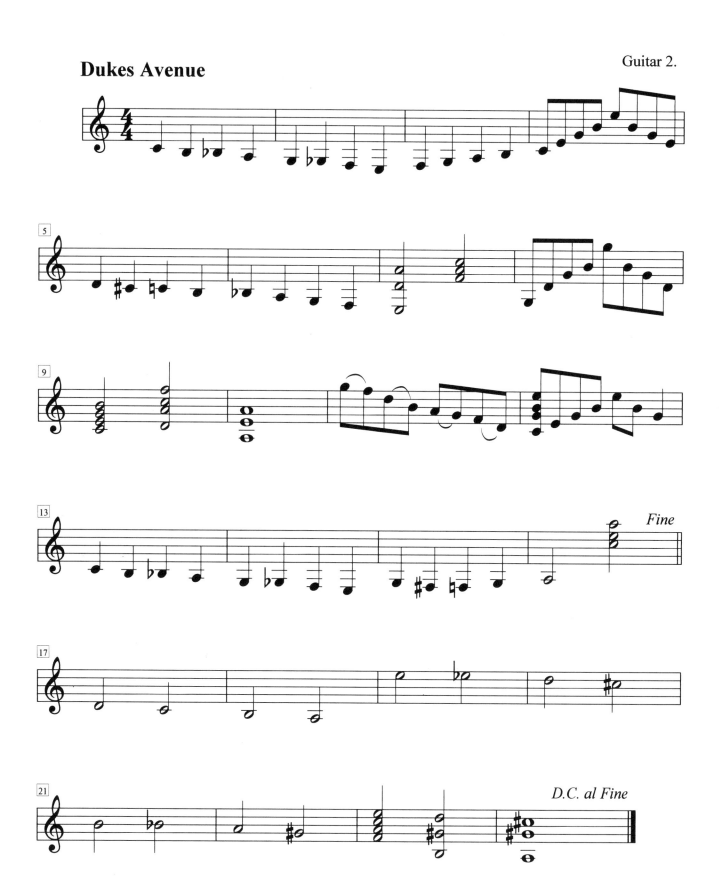

29

Ashbourne Grove

Guitar 1.

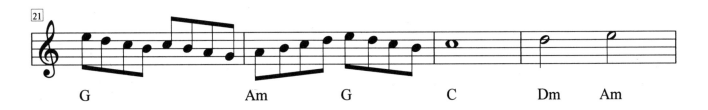

Ashbourne Grove

Guitar 2.

Introduction to $\frac{6}{8}$ Time

$\frac{6}{8}$ is known as 'compound' time because not all of the beats are counted with the same accent. In $\frac{6}{8}$ time, 2 beats are accented in each bar: **1**23 **4**56

1 2 3 **4** 5 6   **1** (2) 3   **4** (5) 6   **1** (2 3) **4** (5) 6   **1** (2 3) **4** (5 6)

Notice how semiquavers ($\frac{1}{16}$ notes) counted in a $\frac{6}{8}$ time are the equivalent of quavers ($\frac{1}{8}$ notes) when counted in a $\frac{4}{4}$ time.

Practise counting this line before trying the following piece:

1 &2& 3   **4**(5) 6   **1**   2   3   **4**(5)& 6

Cross Deep

Guitar 1.

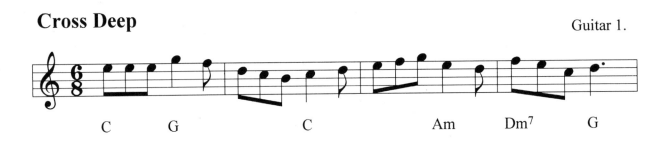

C   G   C   Am   Dm^7 G

C   G   Am   Dm   C   G   Am

Summary of Timing

Here are some semiquavers ($\frac{1}{16}$ notes) in $\frac{6}{8}$ time; they can be counted in different ways:

1 and 2 and 3 **2** 2 (3) **1** and 2 and 3 and **4** 5 6

Notice how semiquavers ($\frac{1}{16}$ notes) differ in the counting of a $\frac{4}{4}$ bar:

1 e & a 2 & 3 4 1 e & a 2 e & 3 (4)

Cross Deep

Guitar 2.

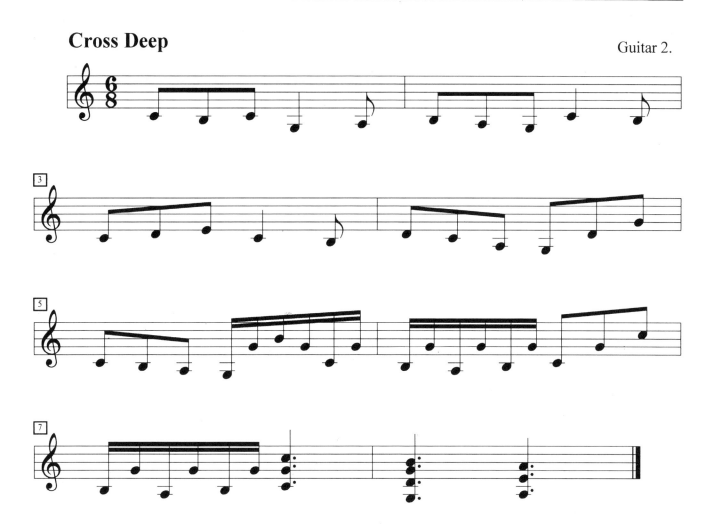

33

4th String Notes

Here are the notes for the 4th string...

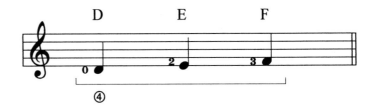

King Street

Guitar 1.

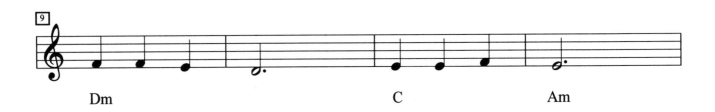

Summary of Notes

Your range of notes for daily practice:

King Street

Guitar 2.

Before you attempt this piece, notice the sign (>) above some of the notes. This means that these notes should be accented (played louder).
Also, try adding expression by following the crescendo (———————) sign – that means play gradually louder.

Shepherds Bush

Guitar 1.

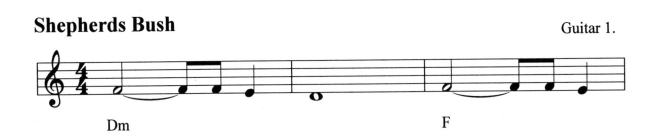

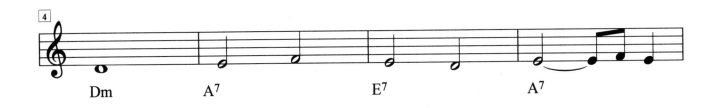

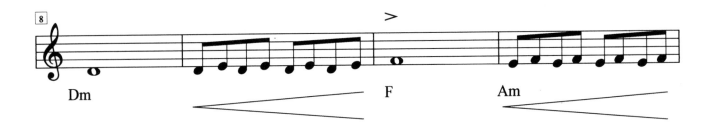

The two vertical dots (:‖) at the end of the music are called 'repeat dots'. They indicate that you should play again from the beginning.

Shepherds Bush

Guitar 2.

Combining Strings 1 to 4

Holland Park

Guitar 1.

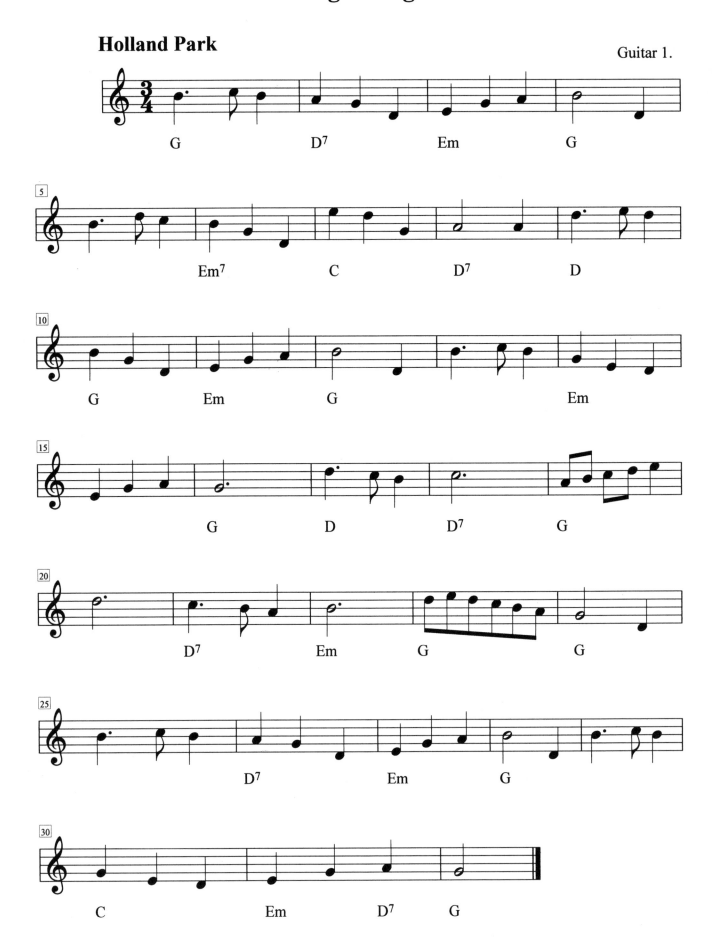

Holland Park

Guitar 2.

5th String Notes

Now we come to the 5th string notes. You will notice that the piece below includes open 4th string notes near the end – but of course you recognise them easily by now. Don't you?!

Here are the notes for the 5th String...

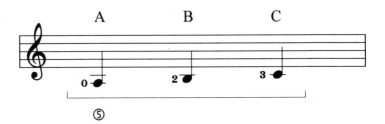

Aubrey Walk

Guitar 1.

Am   E⁷   Am   C

Am   G   C   E⁷

Am

Summary of Notes

Your range of notes now looks like this, and should be played through a number of times at each practice session.

Aubrey Walk

Guitar 2.

Rests

Rests are signs which indicate silence. The duration of each rest is equal to the note of the same name. When a rest appears, count the same value as if you were playing the note.

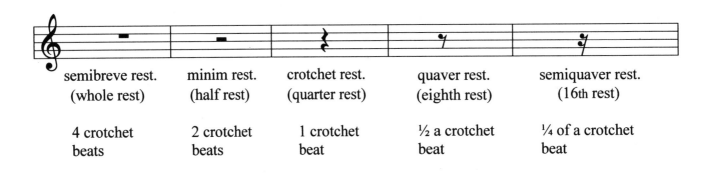

semibreve rest. (whole rest)	minim rest. (half rest)	crotchet rest. (quarter rest)	quaver rest. (eighth rest)	semiquaver rest. (16th rest)
4 crotchet beats	2 crotchet beats	1 crotchet beat	½ a crotchet beat	¼ of a crotchet beat

Sheffield Terrace

Guitar 1.

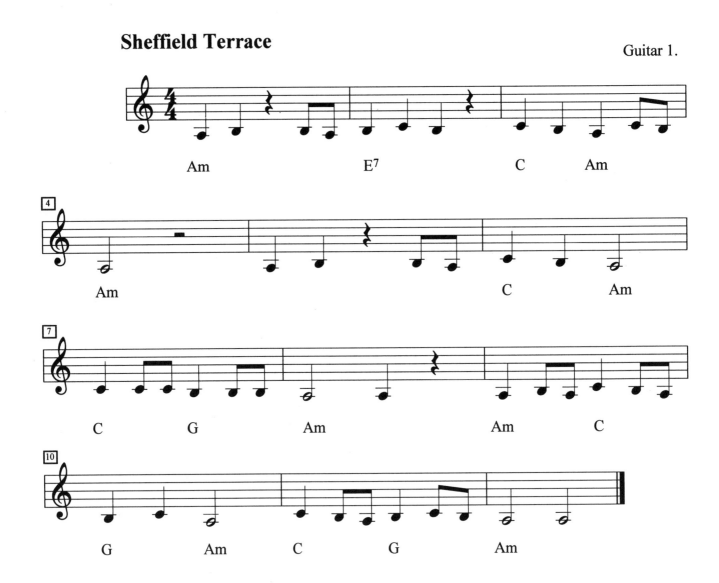

When playing a rest, stop the sound of the strings that were ringing by damping with the right hand.

Practise this exercise below before attempting 'Sheffield Terrace':

Count   1   2 (3   4)   1   (2)   3   (and)   4 e & (a)   1 (2 3 4)
         play   dampen   play   dampen   play   dampen   play   dampen   play and let
                                                                                              ring

Sheffield Terrace

Guitar 2.

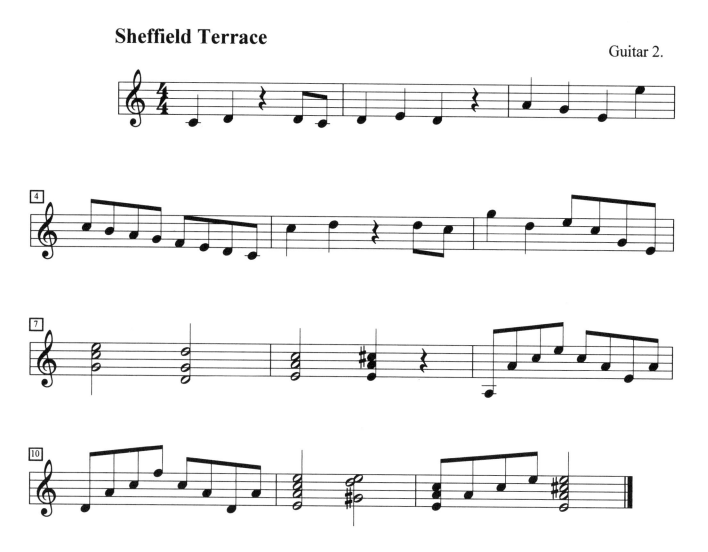

Combining Strings 1 to 5

Notting Hill

Am   Am⁹   D⁷

Am   Dm   F A Dm

G   Dm   C A Am

Am   G   Dm

G   A   Am

Am⁹   G   A

Notting Hill

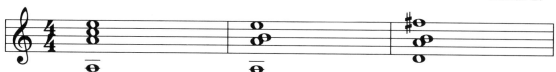

45

Bayswater

Am　　　　　Dm　　　　　Am　　　　　E

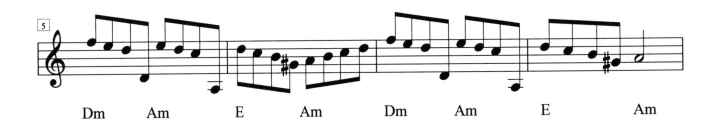

Dm　　Am　　E　　Am　　Dm　　Am　　E　　Am

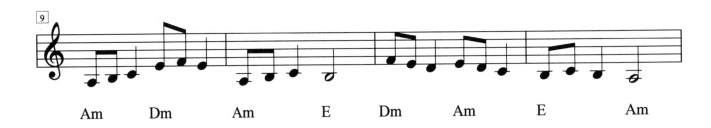

Am　　Dm　　Am　　E　　Dm　　Am　　E　　Am

Am　　　　　Dm　　　　　Am　　　　　E

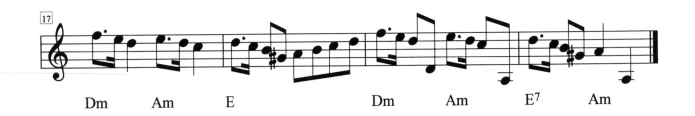

Dm　　Am　　E　　　　　Dm　　Am　　E⁷　　Am

46

Bayswater

Guitar 2.

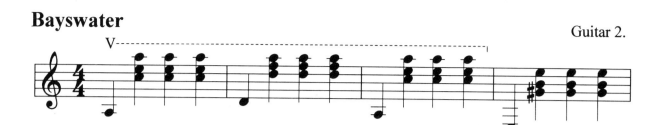

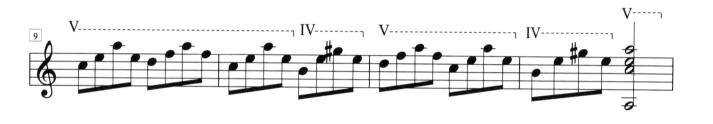

6th String Notes

Here are the notes for the 6th string...

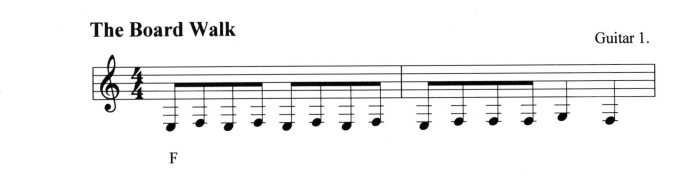

The notes in this piece all look very low, but really it's quite easy.

Start slowly and see if you can play it through perfectly the first time. No cheating now!

The Board Walk

Guitar 1.

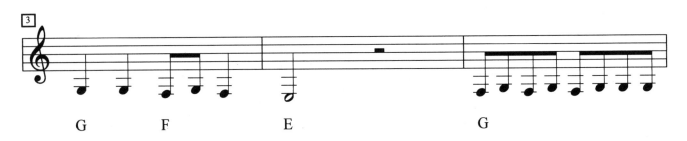

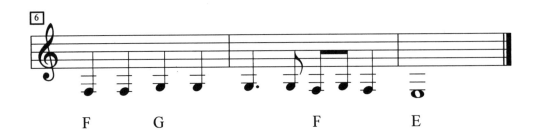

Summary of Ledger Line Notes

Notes extending above or below the stave are written on short lines called ledger lines:

Any bass note NOT on a ledger line is on the 4th string:

Any bass note on or below one ledger line is fretted on the 5th string:

The open 5th string is on the 2nd ledger line:

Any bass note BELOW the 2nd ledger line is on the 6th string:

The Board Walk

Guitar 2.

When you play a semibreve (whole note), keep the fretting finger held down for the whole bar, so that the note sustains and the sound continues (as in bar 4).

When playing notes of different length, be sure that you are PLAYING TO YOUR COUNTING and not fooling yourself by counting to your playing!

Queens Gate Mews

Guitar 1.

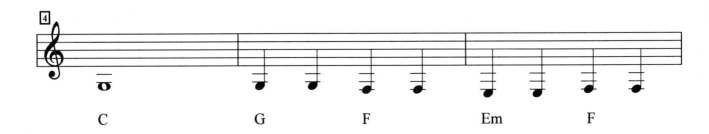

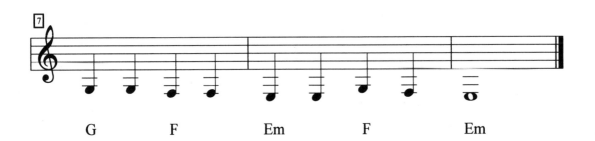

Summary of Notes

Your range of notes for daily practice is now:

Queens Gate Mews

Guitar 2.

Combining Strings 1 to 6

The sign: *rall.* means gradually slow down

Kensington

Guitar 1.

Kensington

Guitar 2.

On the next page is 'The Big One' – 'The Royal Albert Hall' combining all six strings as with this piece. Have fun, and if you have enjoyed getting to the Albert Hall, now's the time to start **'Routes to Sightreading – Book II'**, and who knows where you might end up.

Good Luck,

Chaz Hart

The Royal Albert Hall

Guitar 1.

The Royal Albert Hall

Guitar players – go surfing...